BC 21908

612.8   Wright, Lillian.
Wri
         Smelling and tasting

RAINTREE /STECK-VAUGHN
19903980   CATALOG CARD COMPANY

Smelling
and Tasting

Lillian Wright

RSVP
RAINTREE
STECK-VAUGHN
PUBLISHERS
The Steck-Vaughn Company

Austin, Texas

Series Editor: Pippa Pollard
Science Editor: Kim Merlino
Design: Sally Boothroyd
Project Manager: Julie Klaus
Electronic Production:
    Scott Melcer
Artwork: Mainline Design
Cover Art: Mainline Design

Library of Congress
Cataloging-in-Publication Data

Wright, Lillian.
    Smelling and tasting /
Lillian Wright.
        p.   cm. — (First starts)
    Includes index.
    ISBN 0-8114-5518-1
    1. Smell — Juvenile literature.
2. Taste — Juvenile literature. [1.
Smell.   2. Taste.   3. Senses and
sensation.]   I. Title.   II. Series.
QP456.W75 1995
612.8′6—dc20   94-21454
                                      CIP
                                      AC
Printed and bound in the
United States

1 2 3 4 5 6 7 8 9 0 LB 98 97 96 95 94

Contents

What Are Taste and Smell?

Our senses of taste and smell are less important than our other three senses. Seeing, hearing, and touching help us to find our way around. Tasting and smelling help us to learn more about some objects. They are two closely-related senses. We may get a lot of pleasure from smelling and tasting. But sometimes these are unpleasant experiences.

▽ Our senses of taste and smell give us enjoyment, especially when we eat and drink.

3

A Look at Our Noses

Our noses vary in size, shape, and color. The shape of our nose is inherited. This means it is like our parents' noses. When we press the tip of our nose, we can move it from side to side. The top part near our eyes feels hard. This is because there is bone there to protect the sensitive parts inside. We breathe in air through the two **nostrils**.

▷ Our noses may be large or small, but all are sensitive to smell.

▽ Animals have different nose shapes. The star-nosed mole's nose is very different from ours!

How Do We Smell?

We use our noses to breathe in air. The air carries **odors** that reach the inside of our nose. When this happens, the sensitive part sends messages along the **nerves** to our **brain**. The brain then tells us what we have smelled. When we want to smell something better, we sniff hard. If we hold our nostrils closed, we cannot smell at all.

▷ Some animals are much better at smelling than others The nose of a bloodhound is a thousand times more sensitive than ours.

▽ When we breathe in, the air carries smells into our nose. If we sniff hard, more air can reach the sensitive smell detector parts inside.

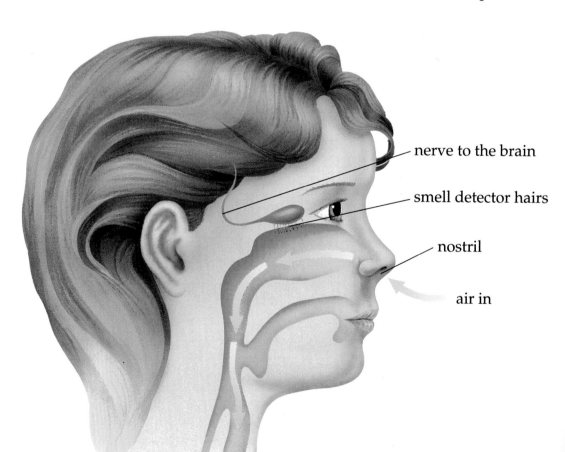

nerve to the brain

smell detector hairs

nostril

air in

Nice and Not So Nice Smells

We do not all like the same odors.
Many people wear perfumes, but there
are thousands of different ones to choose
from. We choose the ones we like. Flowers
and herbs have been used in countries all
around the world to make perfumes and
hide unpleasant odors. Smells that are
familiar to us are often very pleasant.
They can bring back good memories.

▽ A young baby
soon learns the
comforting odor
of its mother.

◁ A substance called incense is burned in many parts of the world to give a pleasing odor.

▷ The musk deer produces musk oil that is used in many expensive perfumes.

Smelling Danger

Some foods smell bad when they rot. This stops us from eating them when they might be harmful to us. The smell of burning tells us that there might be danger. The air carries the odor to our noses and tells us which direction the fire is coming from. This is important for animals, so that they can run to safety. An odor can travel a long distance, especially if a strong wind is blowing.

▽ Animals need their sense of smell to escape danger.

◁ Milk that has turned sour smells unpleasant, so we do not drink it. A really awful smell makes us wrinkle up our nose.

▷ The strong smell of burning food makes us alert to danger.

11

Can We Always Smell?

If we have a cold or hayfever, our sense of smell may not be as good as usual. This is because **mucus** inside our nose stops the smells from reaching the sensitive part inside. Even when our nose is working properly, we do not smell things all the time. When we first go into a room, we may smell someone eating a mint or peeling an orange. But after a while, either our smell sensors stop sending messages, or our brain stops noticing.

▷ Garbage collectors do not notice the smells of the garbage. They get used to these smells.

▽ Hayfever is an allergy caused by the pollen of certain plants. It often causes sneezing and a runny nose. These prevent us from smelling properly. Grasses and herbs like ragweed are often a problem.

Finding Food by Smell

We do not use our sense of smell as much as many animals. But, when we go shopping, we may notice odors coming from different stores. When you are out you can probably tell when you are passing the bakery, a florist, a gas station, a fruit shop, or a fish store. In busy streets you are likely to smell traffic exhaust fumes.

▽ A tiger uses its sense of smell to track down its prey.

▷ Female moths give off a strong **scent** to find a mate. The male can smell this scent trail from as far as 5 miles (8 km) away.

▽ The odor of freshly baked bread stands out.

How Good Is Our Sense of Smell?

As we grow older, we learn the names of many different odors. We have an excellent memory for smell. We may have only smelled a particular odor once, but we are able to recognize it when we smell it again. This may happen many years later. We are also able to smell very small amounts of some substances.

▷ We only have to smell sea air once to remember it.

▽ Vanilla is used to flavor cakes and ice cream. It can be smelled even in small amounts.

How Do We Taste?

When we put some food inside our mouths, we chew it with our teeth. We move it around in our mouths with our tongue and add a watery liquid called **saliva** to it. We are then able to taste it. The taste buds on the tongue send messages along nerves to the brain. Our brain tells us what we can taste and recognizes thousands of different flavors.

▷ Children have more taste buds than adults.

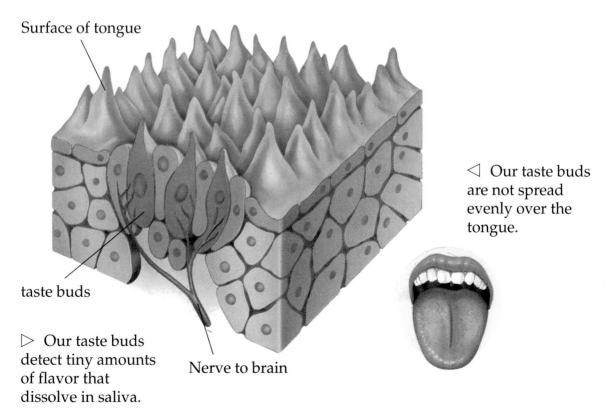

Surface of tongue

taste buds

▷ Our taste buds detect tiny amounts of flavor that dissolve in saliva.

Nerve to brain

◁ Our taste buds are not spread evenly over the tongue.

18

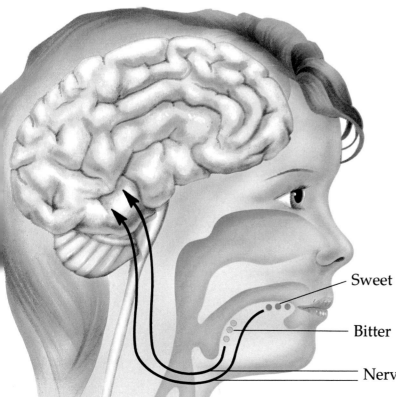

▽ Our brain receives messages from the taste buds and tells us what we have in our mouths. Sensations, such as the sweetness of sugar and the bitterness of coffee, travel to the brain along different nerves. There they are combined to form a single flavor.

Sweet

Bitter

Nerves carrying message to brain

Tasting Carefully

The taste buds on our tongue are sensitive to the tastes of sweet, salt, sour, and bitter. Because we move food around in our mouths, we taste a wide range of flavors. Our sense of smell helps us as well. The odors from food and drinks reach our nose from inside our mouth. So the brain gets messages from nerves about taste and smell at the same time.

▷ When we have a cold, our sense of taste gets no help from our nose.

▷ Our taste buds work together to let us taste different flavors. Sweet and salty flavors are tasted at the front of the tongue, sour at the sides, and bitter at the back. They all work together to let us taste different flavors.

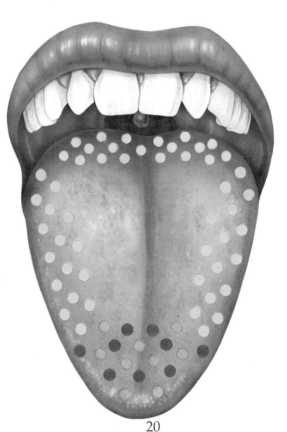

● sweet

● sour

● salty

  bitter

Learning to Taste

When we are young, we learn the taste of many foods. Around the world many different herbs and spices are used to add flavor. Children usually learn to like the flavors given to them by their parents. The texture of the food, whether it feels crunchy or chewy, is also sensed by the tongue. We may dislike some foods because of the way they feel on our tongue and inside our mouth.

▷ These spices are used in dishes around the world to add extra flavor to the food we eat.

▷ Different foods have different textures. Which do you prefer?

▷ Some people have a "sweet tooth," which means that they like sugary foods. But too much sugar can harm the teeth and cause decay. When this happens, a dentist has to remove the decay and fill the tooth. Always brush your teeth after eating to prevent tooth decay.

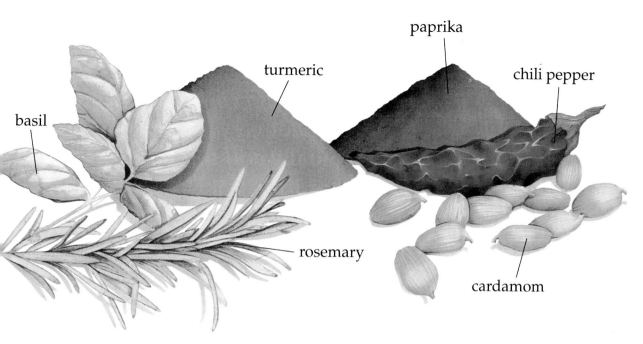

basil

turmeric

rosemary

paprika

chili pepper

cardamom

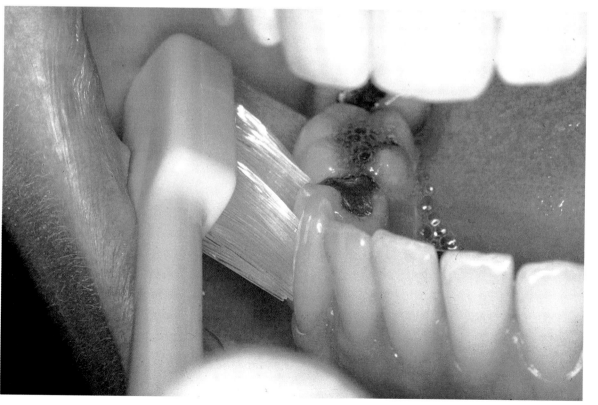

How Good Is Your Sense of Taste?

Some people are more sensitive to taste than others. People who are not very sensitive to sweet tastes usually add more sugar to their cocoa or other hot drinks. People who are more sensitive to salty flavors do not need to add as much salt to their meals as others. Almost everyone finds that a hot drink tastes sweeter than the same drink when it is cold.

▷ A chef seasons a dish carefully with salt and pepper. He does this to bring out the flavor of the food.

▽ Our sense of taste helps us to tell the difference between these pairs of similar foods.

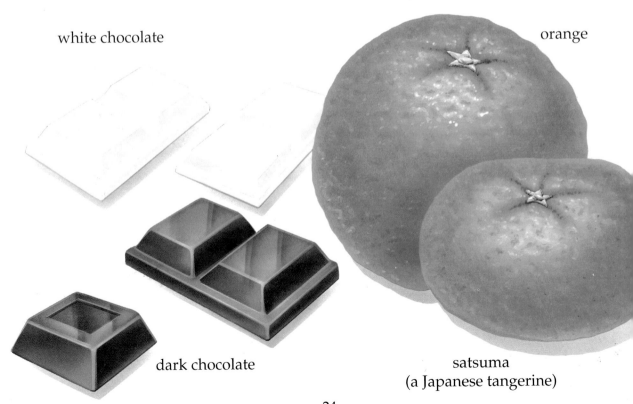

white chocolate

orange

dark chocolate

satsuma
(a Japanese tangerine)

Working with Taste and Smell

Some people use their senses of taste and smell in their work. A **perfumer** has to smell many different scents and choose which ones should be mixed to make a perfume. A coffee taster decides which blend of coffee beans will make the best-selling coffee. Because many animals have a better sense of smell, people train them to help us.

▽ A perfumer mixes scents to make a perfume that people will like.

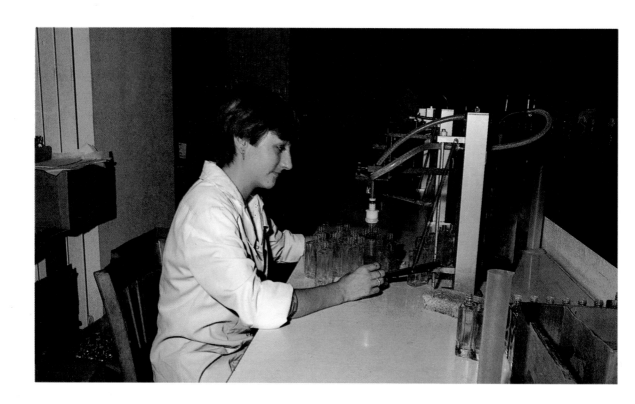

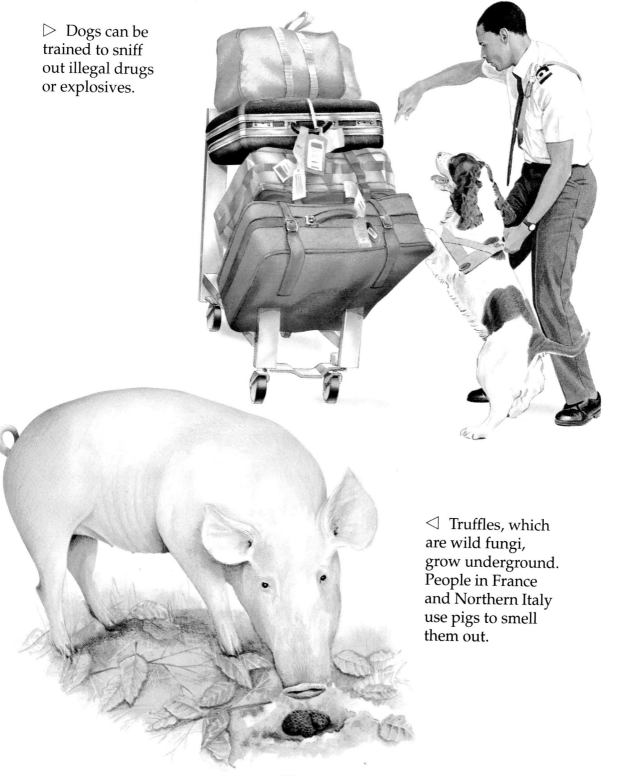

▷ Dogs can be trained to sniff out illegal drugs or explosives.

◁ Truffles, which are wild fungi, grow underground. People in France and Northern Italy use pigs to smell them out.

Animal Noses

For many animals, their senses of taste and smell are very important. They use them to hunt for food, find a mate, and sense when danger is near. But some animals have very special uses for their noses. Their sense of smell works over long distances.

◁ The proboscis monkey has a large nose. Its warning honk can be heard from a distance.

△ Salmon use their sense of smell to swim back to the same stream where they hatched.

▷ The sloth bear eats termites. It closes its nostrils as it pushes its head into a termites' nest. Then it blows the dust away and sucks up the termites.

▽ The Malayan tapir uses its nose, as an extra finger, to pull food toward its mouth.

Things to Do

- See how far away you can smell an object, like a vase of flowers, a plate of food, or an open bottle of perfume.

- Make a pomander, a scented bag or box. Stick cloves into an orange, and allow the orange to dry.

- See if a friend can tell what pieces of food you have put on his or her tongue. Do not let the taster look. First of all, the taster should try without chewing. Then she or he can chew and swallow.

Useful Addresses:

The American Academy of
  Otolaryngology, Head, and
  Neck Surgery
1 Prince Street
Alexandria, VA 22314

Monell Chemical Senses Center
3500 Market Street
Philadelphia, PA 19104

University of Pennsylvania
  Smell and Taste Center
The Hospital of the University
  of Pennsylvania
3400 Spruce Street
Philadelphia, PA 19104

Glossary

brain The organ protected by our skull that receives the messages from the nerves of our body and then tells us what is going on around us.

mucus The sticky liquid produced from inside our nose that helps trap the dirt and germs in the air we breathe and prevents them from entering our body.

nerves Pathways inside our bodies that carry messages from all parts of the body to the brain.

odors Smells carried in the air.

perfumer Someone who makes or sells perfumes.

saliva The watery substance produced inside our mouths. It helps to dissolve food, which allows us to taste it.

scent A smell or odor, often pleasant.

nostrils The two holes at the lower end of our nose. Air gets into our nose through our nostrils.

Index

Photographic credits: British Dental Association 23; Eric Bach/Britstock-1FA 25; Eye Ubiquitous/Suki Coe 19, David Cummings 13, Mike Southern 15; Chris Fairclough Colour Library 3, 5, 21; Robert Harding Picture Library 17; Frank Lane Picture Agency 10; © Michael Habicht/Animals Animals 4; NHPA/Gerard Laez 7; Spectrum Colour Library 26; ZEFA 8, 29.